CW01082857

Juz Amma Dari Kitab Suci Al-Quran Edisi Bahasa Inggris Berwarna Hardcover Version

by

Jannah An-Nur Foundation

2020

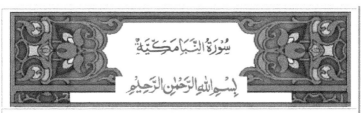

In the name of Allah, Most Gracious, Most Merciful

1. About what are they inquiring.	عَمَّ يَتَسَآءَلُونَ ۞
2. About the great news.	عَنِ النَّبَإِ الْعَظِيمِ ۞
3. That over which they are in disagreement.	الَّذِي هُمْ فِيهِ مُخْتَلِفُونَ ۞
4. Nay, they shall soon know.	كَلَّا سَيَعْلَمُونَ ۞
5. Then nay, they shall soon know.	ثُمَّ كَلَّا سَيَعْلَمُونَ ۞
6. Have We not made the earth a resting place.	أَلَمْ نَجْعَلِ الْأَرْضَ مِهَادًا ۞
7. And the mountains as stakes.	وَالْجِبَالَ أَوْتَادًا ۞
8. And We have created you as pairs.	وَخَلَقْنَاكُمْ أَزْوَاجًا ۞
9. And We have made your sleep (a means) for rest.	وَجَعَلْنَا نَوْمَكُمْ سُبَاتًا ۞
10. And We have made the night as a covering.	وَجَعَلْنَا الَّيْلَ لِبَاسًا ۞
11. And We have made the day for livelihood.	وَجَعَلْنَا النَّهَارَ مَعَاشًا ۞

12. And We have built above you seven strong (heavens).	وَبَنَيْنَا فَوْقَكُمْ سَبْعًا شِدَادًا ۝
13. And We have made a bright, blazing lamp.	وَجَعَلْنَا سِرَاجًا وَهَّاجًا ۝
14. And We have sent down from the rain clouds abundant water.	وَأَنْزَلْنَا مِنَ الْمُعْصِرَاتِ مَاءً ثَجَّاجًا ۝
15. That We may produce thereby grain and vegetation.	لِنُخْرِجَ بِهِ حَبًّا وَنَبَاتًا ۝
16. And gardens of thick growth.	وَجَنَّاتٍ أَلْفَافًا ۝
17. Indeed, the Day of Decision is an appointed time.	إِنَّ يَوْمَ الْفَصْلِ كَانَ مِيقَاتًا ۝
18. The day when the Trumpet is blown, and you shall come forth in multitudes.	يَوْمَ يُنْفَخُ فِي الصُّورِ فَتَأْتُونَ أَفْوَاجًا ۝
19. And the heaven will be opened, so will be as gates.	وَفُتِحَتِ السَّمَاءُ فَكَانَتْ أَبْوَابًا ۝
20. And the mountains are moved, so will be as a mirage.	وَسُيِّرَتِ الْجِبَالُ فَكَانَتْ سَرَابًا ۝
21. Indeed, Hell is a place of ambush.	إِنَّ جَهَنَّمَ كَانَتْ مِرْصَادًا ۝
22. For the rebellious, a dwelling place.	لِلطَّاغِينَ مَآبًا ۝
23. They shall remain lodged therein for ages.	لَابِثِينَ فِيهَا أَحْقَابًا ۝
24. They shall not taste therein any coolness, nor drink.	لَا يَذُوقُونَ فِيهَا بَرْدًا وَلَا شَرَابًا ۝
25. Except boiling water and the discharge from wounds.	إِلَّا حَمِيمًا وَغَسَّاقًا ۝

26. An appropriate recompense.	جَزَآءً وِّفَاقًا ۝
27. Indeed, they were not expecting any reckoning.	اِنَّهُمۡ كَانُوۡا لَا يَرۡجُوۡنَ حِسَابًا ۝
28. And they had denied Our verses as utterly false.	وَّكَذَّبُوۡا بِاٰيٰتِنَا كِذَّابًا ۝
29. And all things have We recorded in a Book.	وَكُلَّ شَىۡءٍ اَحۡصَيۡنٰهُ كِتٰبًا ۝
30. So taste, for We shall never increase you except in torment.	فَذُوۡقُوۡا فَلَنۡ نَّزِيۡدَكُمۡ اِلَّا عَذَابًا ۝
31. Indeed, for the righteous (there is) an abode of success.	اِنَّ لِلۡمُتَّقِيۡنَ مَفَازًا ۝
32. Gardens and grapevines.	حَدَآئِقَ وَاَعۡنَابًا ۝
33. And maidens of equal age.	وَّكَوَاعِبَ اَتۡرَابًا ۝
34. And a full cup.	وَّكَاۡسًا دِهَاقًا ۝
35. They shall not hear therein idle talk, nor falsehood.	لَا يَسۡمَعُوۡنَ فِيۡهَا لَغۡوًا وَّلَا كِذَّابًا ۝
36. A reward from your Lord, a generous gift (due by) account.	جَزَآءً مِّنۡ رَّبِّكَ عَطَآءً حِسَابًا ۝
37. Lord of the heavens and the earth, and whatever is between them, the Beneficent, none can have the power before Him to speak.	رَّبِّ السَّمٰوٰتِ وَالۡاَرۡضِ وَمَا بَيۡنَهُمَا الرَّحۡمٰنِ لَا يَمۡلِكُوۡنَ مِنۡهُ خِطَابًا ۝
38. The Day when the Spirit and the angels shall stand in ranks. They shall not speak except the one whom the Merciful permits, and who speaks what is right.	يَوۡمَ يَقُوۡمُ الرُّوۡحُ وَالۡمَلٰٓئِكَةُ صَفًّا لَا يَتَكَلَّمُوۡنَ اِلَّا مَنۡ اَذِنَ لَهُ الرَّحۡمٰنُ وَقَالَ صَوَابًا ۝

39. That is the True Day. So whoever wills, let him take the path to his Lord.	ذَلِكَ الْيَوْمُ الْحَقُّ ۖ فَمَن شَآءَ اتَّخَذَ إِلَىٰ رَبِّهِ مَآبًا ۞
40. Indeed, We have warned you of the torment near (at hand), the Day when man will see all that his hands have sent forward, and the disbeliever will say: "Would that I were mere dust."	إِنَّا أَنذَرْنَٰكُمْ عَذَابًا قَرِيبًا ۚ يَوْمَ يَنظُرُ الْمَرْءُ مَا قَدَّمَتْ يَدَاهُ وَيَقُولُ الْكَافِرُ يَٰلَيْتَنِى كُنتُ تُرَٰبًا ۞

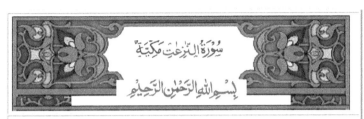

In the name of Allah, Most Gracious, Most Merciful

1. By those (angels) who pull out with violence.	وَالنَّازِعَاتِ غَرْقًا ۞
2. And those who draw out gently.	وَالنَّاشِطَاتِ نَشْطًا ۞
3. And those who glide about swiftly.	وَالسَّابِحَاتِ سَبْحًا ۞
4. Then hasten out as in race (to carry out commands).	فَالسَّابِقَاتِ سَبْقًا ۞
5. Then conduct the affairs.	فَالْمُدَبِّرَاتِ أَمْرًا ۞
6. The Day when the quake shall cause a violent jolt.	يَوْمَ تَرْجُفُ الرَّاجِفَةُ ۞
7. Which is followed by another jolt.	تَتْبَعُهَا الرَّادِفَةُ ۞
8. Hearts on that Day shall tremble with fear.	قُلُوبٌ يَوْمَئِذٍ وَاجِفَةٌ ۞
9. Their eyes humbled.	أَبْصَارُهَا خَاشِعَةٌ ۞
10. They say: "Shall we really be restored to our former state."	يَقُولُونَ أَئِنَّا لَمَرْدُودُونَ فِي الْحَافِرَةِ ۞
11. "What, when we shall have become hollow, rotten bones."	أَئِذَا كُنَّا عِظَامًا نَخِرَةً ۞

12. They say: "It would then be a return with sheer loss."	قَالُوْا تِلْكَ اِذًا كَرَّةٌ خَاسِرَةٌ ۚ۞
13. Then, it would only be a single shout.	فَاِنَّمَا هِىَ زَجْرَةٌ وَّاحِدَةٌ ۙ۞
14. Then they will be suddenly upon the earth alive.	فَاِذَا هُمْ بِالسَّاهِرَةِ ۞
15. Has there reached you the story of Moses.	هَلْ اَتٰىكَ حَدِيْثُ مُوْسٰى ۘ۞
16. When his Lord called out to him in the sacred valley of Tuwa.	اِذْ نَادٰىهُ رَبُّهٗ بِالْوَادِ الْمُقَدَّسِ طُوًى ۚ۞
17. Go to Pharaoh, indeed he has become rebellious.	اِذْهَبْ اِلٰى فِرْعَوْنَ اِنَّهٗ طَغٰى ۖ۞
18. Then say: "Would you purify yourself."	فَقُلْ هَلْ لَّكَ اِلٰى اَنْ تَزَكّٰى ۙ۞
19. "And I may guide you to your Lord, so you may have fear (Him)."	وَاَهْدِيَكَ اِلٰى رَبِّكَ فَتَخْشٰى ۚ۞
20. Then he (Moses) showed him the great sign.	فَاَرٰىهُ الْاٰيَةَ الْكُبْرٰى ۖ۞
21. But he (Pharaoh) denied and disobeyed.	فَكَذَّبَ وَعَصٰى ۖ۞
22. Then, he turned back striving hard.	ثُمَّ اَدْبَرَ يَسْعٰى ۖ۞
23. Then gathered he and summoned.	فَحَشَرَ فَنَادٰى ۖ۞
24. Then he proclaimed: "I am your Lord, the highest."	فَقَالَ اَنَا رَبُّكُمُ الْاَعْلٰى ۖ۞
25. So Allah seized him (and made him) an example for the after (life) and the former.	فَاَخَذَهُ اللّٰهُ نَكَالَ الْاٰخِرَةِ وَالْاُوْلٰى ۗ۞

26. Indeed, in this is a lesson for him who fears.	اِنَّ فِىْ ذٰلِكَ لَعِبْرَةً لِّمَنْ يَّخْشٰى ۗ ﴿٢٦﴾
27. Are you harder to create, or is the heaven, He built it.	ءَاَنْتُمْ اَشَدُّ خَلْقًا اَمِ السَّمَآءُ ۙ بَنٰىهَا ﴿٢٧﴾
28. He raised its vault high, then proportioned it.	رَفَعَ سَمْكَهَا فَسَوّٰىهَا ﴿٢٨﴾
29. And He covered its night (with darkness), and He brought forth its day (with light).	وَاَغْطَشَ لَيْلَهَا وَاَخْرَجَ ضُحٰىهَا ﴿٢٩﴾
30. And after that He spread out the earth.	وَالْاَرْضَ بَعْدَ ذٰلِكَ دَحٰىهَا ﴿٣٠﴾
31. He brought out, from within it, its water and its pasture.	اَخْرَجَ مِنْهَا مَآءَهَا وَمَرْعٰىهَا ﴿٣١﴾
32. And the mountains, He fixed firmly.	وَالْجِبَالَ اَرْسٰىهَا ﴿٣٢﴾
33. A sustenance for you and for your cattle.	مَتَاعًا لَّكُمْ وَلِاَنْعَامِكُمْ ﴿٣٣﴾
34. Then, when there comes the greatest catastrophe.	فَاِذَا جَآءَتِ الطَّآمَّةُ الْكُبْرٰى ﴿٣٤﴾
35. The Day when man shall remember what he strove for.	يَوْمَ يَتَذَكَّرُ الْاِنْسَانُ مَا سَعٰى ﴿٣٥﴾
36. And Hell shall be laid open for (every) one who sees.	وَبُرِّزَتِ الْجَحِيْمُ لِمَنْ يَّرٰى ﴿٣٦﴾
37. Then as for him who had rebelled.	فَاَمَّا مَنْ طَغٰى ﴿٣٧﴾
38. And preferred the life of the world.	وَاٰثَرَ الْحَيٰوةَ الدُّنْيَا ﴿٣٨﴾
39. Then indeed, Hell shall be his abode.	فَاِنَّ الْجَحِيْمَ هِيَ الْمَاْوٰى ﴿٣٩﴾

40. And as for him who had feared to stand before his Lord and restrained himself from evil desires.	وَأَمَّا مَنْ خَافَ مَقَامَ رَبِّهِ وَنَهَى النَّفْسَ عَنِ الْهَوَى ۞
41. Then indeed, Paradise shall be his abode.	فَإِنَّ الْجَنَّةَ هِيَ الْمَأْوَى ۞
42. They ask you (O Muhammad), about the Hour. When is its appointed time.	يَسْأَلُونَكَ عَنِ السَّاعَةِ أَيَّانَ مُرْسَاهَا ۞
43. In what (position) are you to mention of it.	فِيمَ أَنْتَ مِنْ ذِكْرَاهَا ۞
44. With your Lord is the (knowledge) term thereof.	إِلَى رَبِّكَ مُنْتَهَاهَا ۞
45. You are only a warner (to him) who fears it.	إِنَّمَا أَنْتَ مُنْذِرُ مَنْ يَخْشَاهَا ۞
46. On the day when they see it, it will be as if they had not stayed except for an evening or the morning thereof.	كَأَنَّهُمْ يَوْمَ يَرَوْنَهَا لَمْ يَلْبَثُوا إِلَّا عَشِيَّةً أَوْ ضُحَاهَا ۞

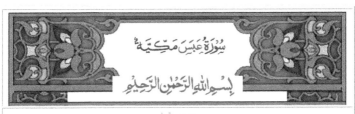

In the name of Allah, Most Gracious, Most Merciful

1. He frowned and turned away.	عَبَسَ وَتَوَلَّىٰ ۞
2. Because there came to him the blind man.	اَنْ جَآءَهُ الْاَعْمٰىٰ ۞
3. And what would make you know that he might be purified.	وَمَا يُدْرِيكَ لَعَلَّهُ يَزَّكَّىٰ ۞
4. Or be reminded, then might benefit him the reminding.	اَوْ يَذَّكَّرُ فَتَنْفَعَهُ الذِّكْرَىٰ ۞
5. As for him who thinks himself self-sufficient.	اَمَّا مَنِ اسْتَغْنَىٰ ۞
6. Then to him you give attention.	فَاَنْتَ لَهُ تَصَدَّىٰ ۞
7. And no (blame) upon you if he is not purified.	وَمَا عَلَيْكَ اَلَّا يَزَّكَّىٰ ۞
8. And as for him who came to you striving (for knowledge).	وَاَمَّا مَنْ جَآءَكَ يَسْعَىٰ ۞
9. And he fears (Allah).	وَهُوَ يَخْشَىٰ ۞
10. So from him you are distracted.	فَاَنْتَ عَنْهُ تَلَهَّىٰ ۞
11. Nay, indeed, they (verses of Quran) are a reminder.	كَلَّا اِنَّهَا تَذْكِرَةٌ ۞

12. So whoever wills, let him remember it.	فَمَن شَآءَ ذَكَرَهُ ۞
13. (Recorded) in honored scrolls.	فِى صُحُفٍ مُّكَرَّمَةٍ ۞
14. Exalted, purified.	مَّرْفُوعَةٍ مُّطَهَّرَةٍ ۞
15. In the hands of scribes (angels).	بِأَيْدِى سَفَرَةٍ ۞
16. Noble, virtuous.	كِرَامٍ بَرَرَةٍ ۞
17. Be destroyed man, how ungrateful he is.	قُتِلَ الْإِنسَانُ مَآ أَكْفَرَهُ ۞
18. From what did He create him.	مِنْ أَىِّ شَىْءٍ خَلَقَهُ ۞
19. From a sperm drop. He created him, then set him his destiny.	مِن نُّطْفَةٍ خَلَقَهُ فَقَدَّرَهُ ۞
20. Then He made the way easy for him.	ثُمَّ السَّبِيلَ يَسَّرَهُ ۞
21. Then He caused him to die, and brought him to the grave.	ثُمَّ أَمَاتَهُ فَأَقْبَرَهُ ۞
22. Then when He wills. He will resurrect him.	ثُمَّ إِذَا شَآءَ أَنشَرَهُ ۞
23. Nay, he (man) has not done what He commanded him.	كَلَّا لَمَّا يَقْضِ مَآ أَمَرَهُ ۞
24. Then let man look at his food.	فَلْيَنظُرِ الْإِنسَانُ إِلَى طَعَامِهِ ۞
25. That We poured down water in abundance.	أَنَّا صَبَبْنَا الْمَآءَ صَبًّا ۞
26. Then We split the earth in clefts.	ثُمَّ شَقَقْنَا الْأَرْضَ شَقًّا ۞

27. Then caused to grow within it grain.	فَأَنۢبَتۡنَا فِيهَا حَبًّا ۝
28. And grapes and vegetables.	وَّعِنَبًا وَّقَضۡبًا ۝
29. And olives and dates.	وَّزَيۡتُونًا وَّنَخۡلًا ۝
30. And lush gardens.	وَّحَدَآئِقَ غُلۡبًا ۝
31. And fruits and fodder.	وَّفَاكِهَةً وَّأَبًّا ۝
32. A sustenance for you and your cattle.	مَّتَاعًا لَّكُمۡ وَلِأَنۡعَامِكُمۡ ۝
33. Then when the deafening blast comes.	فَإِذَا جَآءَتِ الصَّآخَّةُ ۝
34. That Day shall man flee from his brother.	يَوۡمَ يَفِرُّ الۡمَرۡءُ مِنۡ أَخِيهِ ۝
35. And his mother and his father.	وَأُمِّهِ وَأَبِيهِ ۝
36. And his wife and his children.	وَصَاحِبَتِهِ وَبَنِيهِ ۝
37. Each one of them, on that Day, shall have enough to make him heedless of others.	لِكُلِّ امۡرِئٍ مِّنۡهُمۡ يَوۡمَئِذٍ شَأۡنٌ يُغۡنِيهِ ۝
38. (Some) faces, that Day, shall be bright.	وُجُوهٌ يَوۡمَئِذٍ مُّسۡفِرَةٌ ۝
39. Rejoicing and joyful.	ضَاحِكَةٌ مُّسۡتَبۡشِرَةٌ ۝
40. And (other) faces, that Day, shall have dust upon them.	وَوُجُوهٌ يَوۡمَئِذٍ عَلَيۡهَا غَبَرَةٌ ۝
41. Darkness covering them.	تَرۡهَقُهَا قَتَرَةٌ ۝

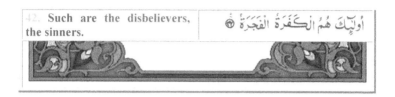

42. Such are the disbelievers, the sinners.

أُولَٰئِكَ هُمُ الْكَفَرَةُ الْفَجَرَةُ ۝

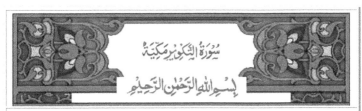

AtTakweer

In the name of Allah, Most Gracious, Most Merciful

1. When the sun is folded up.	إِذَا الشَّمْسُ كُوِّرَتْ ۝
2. And when the stars scatter.	وَإِذَا النُّجُومُ انكَدَرَتْ ۝
3. And when the mountains are set in motion.	وَإِذَا الْجِبَالُ سُيِّرَتْ ۝
4. And when the full term she camels are left untended.	وَإِذَا الْعِشَارُ عُطِّلَتْ ۝
5. And when the wild beasts are gathered together.	وَإِذَا الْوُحُوشُ حُشِرَتْ ۝
6. And when the oceans are set ablaze.	وَإِذَا الْبِحَارُ سُجِّرَتْ ۝
7. And when the souls are re-united (with the bodies).	وَإِذَا النُّفُوسُ زُوِّجَتْ ۝
8. And when the infant girl, buried alive, is asked.	وَإِذَا الْمَوْءُودَةُ سُئِلَتْ ۝
9. For what sin she was killed.	بِأَيِّ ذَنبٍ قُتِلَتْ ۝
10. And when the records are unfolded.	وَإِذَا الصُّحُفُ نُشِرَتْ ۝
11. And when the sky is torn away.	وَإِذَا السَّمَاءُ كُشِطَتْ ۝

12. And when Hell is set ablaze.	وَإِذَا الْجَحِيمُ سُعِّرَتْ ۞
13. And when Paradise is brought near.	وَإِذَا الْجَنَّةُ أُزْلِفَتْ ۞
14. A soul (then) shall know what it has brought with him.	عَلِمَتْ نَفْسٌ مَّا أَحْضَرَتْ ۞
15. Nay, so I swear by the retreating stars.	فَلَا أُقْسِمُ بِالْخُنَّسِ ۞
16. (The stars which) move swiftly and disappear.	الْجَوَارِ الْكُنَّسِ ۞
17. And the night when it departs.	وَالَّيْلِ إِذَا عَسْعَسَ ۞
18. And the dawn when it breathes up.	وَالصُّبْحِ إِذَا تَنَفَّسَ ۞
19. Indeed, this is the word (brought) by a noble messenger.	إِنَّهُ لَقَوْلُ رَسُولٍ كَرِيمٍ ۞
20. Owner of power, secure with the Owner of the Throne.	ذِى قُوَّةٍ عِندَ ذِى الْعَرْشِ مَكِينٍ ۞
21. He is obeyed and (held as) trustworthy.	مُّطَاعٍ ثَمَّ أَمِينٍ ۞
22. And your Companion (Muhammad) is not a madman.	وَمَا صَاحِبُكُم بِمَجْنُونٍ ۞
23. And indeed, he has seen him on the clear horizon.	وَلَقَدْ رَآهُ بِالْأُفُقِ الْمُبِينِ ۞
24. And he is not a withholder (of knowledge) of the unseen.	وَمَا هُوَ عَلَى الْغَيْبِ بِضَنِينٍ ۞
25. And this is not the word of an accursed Satan.	وَمَا هُوَ بِقَوْلِ شَيْطَانٍ رَّجِيمٍ ۞
26. Where then are you going.	فَأَيْنَ تَذْهَبُونَ ۞

27. This is not else than a reminder to the worlds.	اِنْ هُوَ اِلَّا ذِكْرٌ لِّلْعٰلَمِيْنَ ۞
28. For whoever wills among you to take a straight path.	لِمَنْ شَآءَ مِنْكُمْ اَنْ يَّسْتَقِيْمَ ۞
29. And you do not will, except that Allah wills, Lord of the worlds.	وَمَا تَشَآءُوْنَ اِلَّا اَنْ يَّشَآءَ اللّٰهُ رَبُّ الْعٰلَمِيْنَ ۞

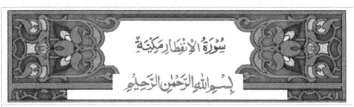

In the name of Allah, Most Gracious, Most Merciful

In the name of Allah, Most Gracious, Most Merciful

1. When the heaven splits asunder.	اِذَا السَّمَاءُ انْفَطَرَتْ ۞
2. And when the stars scatter.	وَاِذَا الْكَوَاكِبُ انْتَثَرَتْ ۞
3. And when the seas are erupted.	وَاِذَا الْبِحَارُ فُجِّرَتْ ۞
4. And when the graves are turned upside down.	وَاِذَا الْقُبُوْرُ بُعْثِرَتْ ۞
5. A soul shall know what it has sent forward and (what it has) left behind.	عَلِمَتْ نَفْسٌ مَّا قَدَّمَتْ وَاَخَّرَتْ ۞
6. O mankind, what has deceived you concerning your Lord, the Gracious.	يٰۤاَيُّهَا الْاِنْسَانُ مَا غَرَّكَ بِرَبِّكَ الْكَرِيْمِ ۞
7. He who created you, then He fashioned you, then He proportioned you.	الَّذِيْ خَلَقَكَ فَسَوّٰىكَ فَعَدَلَكَ ۞
8. In whatever form He willed, He put you together.	فِيْۤ اَيِّ صُوْرَةٍ مَّا شَاءَ رَكَّبَكَ ۞
9. Nay, but you deny the (Day of) rewards and punishments.	كَلَّا بَلْ تُكَذِّبُوْنَ بِالدِّيْنِ ۞

10. And indeed, there are above you guardians.	وَإِنَّ عَلَيْكُمْ لَحَٰفِظِينَ ۝
11. Honorable scribes.	كِرَامًا كَٰتِبِينَ ۝
12. They know whatever you do.	يَعْلَمُونَ مَا تَفْعَلُونَ ۝
13. Indeed, the righteous shall be in delight.	إِنَّ الْأَبْرَارَ لَفِى نَعِيمٍ ۝
14. And indeed, the wicked shall be in Hellfire.	وَإِنَّ الْفُجَّارَ لَفِى جَحِيمٍ ۝
15. They shall (enter to) burn in it on the Day of Recompense.	يَصْلَوْنَهَا يَوْمَ الدِّينِ ۝
16. And they shall never be absent from it.	وَمَا هُمْ عَنْهَا بِغَآئِبِينَ ۝
17. And what do you know what the Day of Recompense is.	وَمَآ أَدْرَىٰكَ مَا يَوْمُ الدِّينِ ۝
18. Then, what do you know what the Day of Recompense is.	ثُمَّ مَآ أَدْرَىٰكَ مَا يَوْمُ الدِّينِ ۝
19. A Day when no soul shall have the power to do anything for another soul. And the command that Day is with Allah.	يَوْمَ لَا تَمْلِكُ نَفْسٌ لِّنَفْسٍ شَيْئًا ۖ وَالْأَمْرُ يَوْمَئِذٍ لِّلَّهِ ۝

AlMutaffifin

In the name of Allah, Most Gracious, Most Merciful

1. Woe to those who give less in weight.	وَيْلٌ لِّلْمُطَفِّفِينَ ۞
2. Those who, when they take by measure from people, take in full.	الَّذِينَ إِذَا اكْتَالُوا عَلَى النَّاسِ يَسْتَوْفُونَ ۞
3. And when they give by measure or weigh for them, they cause loss.	وَإِذَا كَالُوهُمْ أَوْ وَزَنُوهُمْ يُخْسِرُونَ ۞
4. Do such (people) not think that they will be raised again.	أَلَا يَظُنُّ أُولَٰئِكَ أَنَّهُم مَّبْعُوثُونَ ۞
5. On a Great Day.	لِيَوْمٍ عَظِيمٍ ۞
6. The Day when mankind shall stand before the Lord of the worlds.	يَوْمَ يَقُومُ النَّاسُ لِرَبِّ الْعَالَمِينَ ۞
7. Nay, indeed, the record of the wicked is in sijjeen.	كَلَّا إِنَّ كِتَابَ الْفُجَّارِ لَفِي سِجِّينٍ ۞
8. And what do you know what sijjeen is.	وَمَا أَدْرَاكَ مَا سِجِّينٌ ۞
9. (It is) a written record.	كِتَابٌ مَّرْقُومٌ ۞

10. Woe that Day to the deniers.	وَيْلٌ يَّوْمَئِذٍ لِّلْمُكَذِّبِيْنَ ۟
11. Those who deny the Day of Recompense.	الَّذِيْنَ يُكَذِّبُوْنَ بِيَوْمِ الدِّيْنِ ۟
12. And none denies it except every sinful transgressor.	وَمَا يُكَذِّبُ بِهٖ اِلَّا كُلُّ مُعْتَدٍ اَثِيْمٍ۟
13. When Our verses are recited to him, he says: "Tales of the ancient peoples."	اِذَا تُتْلٰى عَلَيْهِ اٰيٰتُنَا قَالَ اَسَاطِيْرُ الْاَوَّلِيْنَ۟
14. Nay, but upon their hearts is rust of that which they have earned.	كَلَّا بَلْ رَانَ عَلٰى قُلُوْبِهِمْ مَّا كَانُوْا يَكْسِبُوْنَ۟
15. Nay, indeed, they shall be debarred, on that Day, from (the mercy of) their Lord.	كَلَّا اِنَّهُمْ عَنْ رَّبِّهِمْ يَوْمَئِذٍ لَّمَحْجُوْبُوْنَ۟
16. Then surely they shall (enter to) burn in Hellfire.	ثُمَّ اِنَّهُمْ لَصَالُوا الْجَحِيْمِ۟
17. Then it will be said: "This is what you used to deny."	ثُمَّ يُقَالُ هٰذَا الَّذِيْ كُنْتُمْ بِهٖ تُكَذِّبُوْنَ۟
18. Nay, indeed, the record of the righteous is in illiyeen.	كَلَّا اِنَّ كِتٰبَ الْاَبْرَارِ لَفِيْ عِلِّيِّيْنَ۟
19. And what do you know what illiyuun is.	وَمَا اَدْرٰىكَ مَا عِلِّيُّوْنَ۟
20. (It is) a written record.	كِتٰبٌ مَّرْقُوْمٌ۟
21. It is witnessed by those brought near (to Allah).	يَّشْهَدُهُ الْمُقَرَّبُوْنَ۟
22. Indeed, the righteous shall be in delight.	اِنَّ الْاَبْرَارَ لَفِيْ نَعِيْمٍ۟

23. On high couches they shall be looking.	عَلَى الْأَرَآئِكِ يَنْظُرُونَ ۝
24. You shall recognize in their faces the radiance of delight.	تَعْرِفُ فِى وُجُوهِهِمْ نَضْرَةَ النَّعِيمِ ۝
25. They shall be given to drink of a pure wine, sealed.	يُسْقَوْنَ مِنْ رَّحِيقٍ مَّخْتُومٍ ۝
26. Whose seal is musk. And for this let them strive, those who want to strive.	خِتَـمُهُ مِسْكٌ وَفِى ذَلِكَ فَلْيَتَنَافَسِ الْمُتَنَافِسُونَ ۝
27. And that (wine) shall have the mixture of Tasneem.	وَمِزَاجُهُ مِنْ تَسْنِيمٍ ۝
28. A spring from which those near (to Allah) shall drink.	عَيْنًا يَّشْرَبُ بِهَا الْمُقَرَّبُونَ ۝
29. Indeed, those who committed crimes used to laugh at those who believed.	إِنَّ الَّذِينَ أَجْرَمُوا كَانُوا مِنَ الَّذِينَ أَمَنُوا يَضْحَكُونَ ۝
30. And when they passed by them, they would wink at one another.	وَإِذَا مَرُّوا بِهِمْ يَتَغَامَزُونَ ۝
31. And when they returned to their own folk, they would return jesting.	وَإِذَا انْقَلَبُوا إِلَى أَهْلِهِمُ انْقَلَبُوا فَكِهِينَ ۝
32. And when they saw them, they would say: "Surely, these are (the people) gone astray."	وَإِذَا رَأَوْهُمْ قَالُوا إِنَّ هَؤُلَاءِ لَضَآلُّونَ ۝
33. And they had not been sent to be guardians over them.	وَمَآ أُرْسِلُوا عَلَيْهِمْ حَفِظِينَ ۝

34. So today those who believed are laughing at the disbelievers.	فَالْيَوْمَ الَّذِينَ اٰمَنُوْا مِنَ الْكُفَّارِ يَضْحَكُوْنَ ۞
35. On high couches they shall be looking.	عَلَى الْاَرَآئِكِ يَنْظُرُوْنَ ۞
36. Have the disbelievers (not) been duly rewarded for what they used to do.	هَلْ ثُوِّبَ الْكُفَّارُ مَا كَانُوْا يَفْعَلُوْنَ ۞

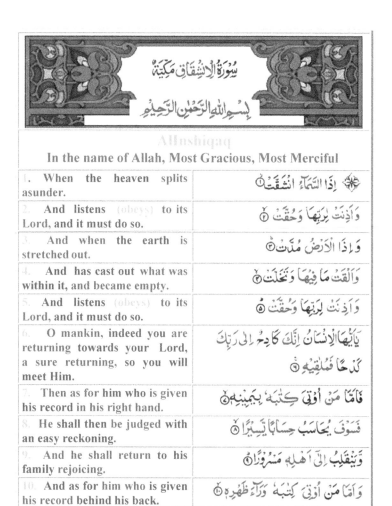

سُوْرَةُ الْاِنْشِقَاقِ مَكِّيَّةٌ

بِسْمِ اللهِ الرَّحْمٰنِ الرَّحِيْمِ

In the name of Allah, Most Gracious, Most Merciful

1. When the heaven splits asunder.	﴿١﴾ اِذَا السَّمَآءُ انْشَقَّتْ
2. And listens (obeys) to its Lord, and it must do so.	وَاَذِنَتْ لِرَبِّهَا وَحُقَّتْ ﴿٢﴾
3. And when the earth is stretched out.	وَاِذَا الْاَرْضُ مُدَّتْ ﴿٣﴾
4. And has cast out what was within it, and became empty.	وَاَلْقَتْ مَا فِيْهَا وَتَخَلَّتْ ﴿٤﴾
5. And listens (obeys) to its Lord, and it must do so.	وَاَذِنَتْ لِرَبِّهَا وَحُقَّتْ ﴿٥﴾
6. O mankin, indeed you are returning towards your Lord, a sure returning, so you will meet Him.	يٰۤاَيُّهَا الْاِنْسَانُ اِنَّكَ كَادِحٌ اِلٰى رَبِّكَ كَدْحًا فَمُلٰقِيْهِ ﴿٦﴾
7. Then as for him who is given his record in his right hand.	فَاَمَّا مَنْ اُوْتِيَ كِتٰبَهُ بِيَمِيْنِهٖ ﴿٧﴾
8. He shall then be judged with an easy reckoning.	فَسَوْفَ يُحَاسَبُ حِسَابًا يَّسِيْرًا ﴿٨﴾
9. And he shall return to his family rejoicing.	وَيَنْقَلِبُ اِلٰۤى اَهْلِهٖ مَسْرُوْرًا ﴿٩﴾
10. And as for him who is given his record behind his back.	وَاَمَّا مَنْ اُوْتِيَ كِتٰبَهُ وَرَآءَ ظَهْرِهٖ ﴿١٠﴾

11. He shall call for death.	فَسَوْفَ يَدْعُوْا ثُبُوْرًا ۚ ۞
12. And he shall (enter to) burn in a blazing Fire.	وَّيَصْلٰى سَعِيْرًا ۞
13. Indeed, He had been among his family in joy.	اِنَّهٗ كَانَ فِيْۤ اَهْلِهٖ مَسْرُوْرًا ۞
14. Indeed, he thought that he would never return (to Allah).	اِنَّهٗ ظَنَّ اَنْ لَّنْ يَّحُوْرَ ۞
15. But yes, indeed, His Lord was ever watching him.	بَلٰى ۚ اِنَّ رَبَّهٗ كَانَ بِهٖ بَصِيْرًا ۞
16. So no, I swear by the twilight.	فَلَاۤ اُقْسِمُ بِالشَّفَقِ ۞
17. And the night and what it gathers.	وَالَّيْلِ وَمَا وَسَقَ ۞
18. And the moon when it becomes full.	وَالْقَمَرِ اِذَا اتَّسَقَ ۞
19. That you will surely embark upon state after state.	لَتَرْكَبُنَّ طَبَقًا عَنْ طَبَقٍ ۞
20. Then, what is (the matter) with them, they do not believe.	فَمَا لَهُمْ لَا يُؤْمِنُوْنَ ۞
21. And when the Quran is recited to them, they do not fall prostrate. **AsSajda**	وَاِذَا قُرِئَ عَلَيْهِمُ الْقُرْاٰنُ لَا يَسْجُدُوْنَ ۞ ۩
22. But those who disbelieve, they deny.	بَلِ الَّذِيْنَ كَفَرُوْا يُكَذِّبُوْنَ ۞
23. Although Allah knows best what they are gathering.	وَاللّٰهُ اَعْلَمُ بِمَا يُوْعُوْنَ ۞
24. So, give them the tidings of a painful punishment.	فَبَشِّرْهُمْ بِعَذَابٍ اَلِيْمٍ ۞

25. Except for those who believe and do righteous deeds, for them is a reward uninterrupted.

إِلَّا الَّذِينَ اٰمَنُوْا وَعَمِلُوا الصّٰلِحٰتِ لَهُمْ اَجْرٌ غَيْرُ مَمْنُوْنٍ ۝

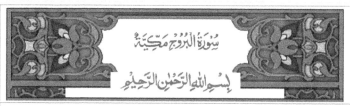

سُورَةُ الْبُرُوجِ مَكِّيَّةٌ

بِسْمِ اللهِ الرَّحْمٰنِ الرَّحِيْمِ

In the name of Allah, Most Gracious, Most Merciful

1. By the heaven with mansions of stars.	وَالسَّمَآءِ ذَاتِ الْبُرُوْجِ ۝
2. And the promised Day.	وَالْيَوْمِ الْمَوْعُوْدِ ۝
3. And the witness and that which is witnessed.	وَشَاهِدٍ وَّمَشْهُوْدٍ ۝
4. Destroyed were the people of the ditch.	قُتِلَ اَصْحٰبُ الْاُخْدُوْدِ ۝
5. Of the fire fed by the blazing fuel.	النَّارِ ذَاتِ الْوَقُوْدِ ۝
6. When they were sitting by it.	اِذْهُمْ عَلَيْهَا قُعُوْدٌ ۝
7. And they, to what they were doing with the believers, were themselves witnesses.	وَّهُمْ عَلٰى مَا يَفْعَلُوْنَ بِالْمُؤْمِنِيْنَ شُهُوْدٌ ۝
8. And they resented them not except that they had believed in Allah, the All Mighty, the Self Praiseworthy.	وَمَا نَقَمُوْا مِنْهُمْ اِلَّآ اَنْ يُّؤْمِنُوْا بِاللهِ الْعَزِيْزِ الْحَمِيْدِ ۝

9. Who, to Whom belongs the dominion of the heavens and the earth. And Allah is Witness over everything.	الَّذِىْ لَهٗ مُلْكُ السَّمٰوٰتِ وَالْاَرْضِ ۭ وَاللّٰهُ عَلٰى كُلِّ شَىْءٍ شَهِيْدٌ ۞
10. Indeed, those who put into trial the believing men and the believing women, and then did not repent (of it), for them is the punishment of Hell, and for them is the punishment of burning.	اِنَّ الَّذِيْنَ فَتَنُوا الْمُؤْمِنِيْنَ وَالْمُؤْمِنٰتِ ثُمَّ لَمْ يَتُوْبُوْا فَلَهُمْ عَذَابُ جَهَنَّمَ وَلَهُمْ عَذَابُ الْحَرِيْقِ ۞
11. Indeed, those who believed and did righteous deeds, for them are Gardens beneath which rivers flow. This is the supreme success.	اِنَّ الَّذِيْنَ اٰمَنُوْا وَعَمِلُوا الصّٰلِحٰتِ لَهُمْ جَنّٰتٌ تَجْرِىْ مِنْ تَحْتِهَا الْاَنْهٰرُ ۭ ذٰلِكَ الْفَوْزُ الْكَبِيْرُ ۞
12. Indeed, the grip of your Lord is very severe.	اِنَّ بَطْشَ رَبِّكَ لَشَدِيْدٌ ۞
13. Indeed, it is He Who originates, and will repeat (create again).	اِنَّهٗ هُوَ يُبْدِئُ وَيُعِيْدُ ۞
14. And He is the All Forgiving, the All Loving.	وَهُوَ الْغَفُوْرُ الْوَدُوْدُ ۞
15. Owner of the Throne, the Exalted.	ذُو الْعَرْشِ الْمَجِيْدُ ۞
16. Doer of whatever He intends.	فَعَّالٌ لِّمَا يُرِيْدُ ۞
17. Has there reached you the story of the hosts.	هَلْ اَتٰىكَ حَدِيْثُ الْجُنُوْدِ ۞

18. Pharaoh and Thamud.	فِرْعَوْنَ وَثَمُوْدَ ۞
19. But those who disbelieve, persist in denying.	بَلِ الَّذِيْنَ كَفَرُوْا فِيْ تَكْذِيْبٍ ۞
20. While Allah has encircled them from behind.	وَّاللّٰهُ مِنْ وَّرَآئِهِمْ مُّحِيْطٌ ۞
21. Nay, but this is a glorious Quran.	بَلْ هُوَ قُرْاٰنٌ مَّجِيْدٌ ۞
22. In the guarded tablet.	فِيْ لَوْحٍ مَّحْفُوْظٍ ۞

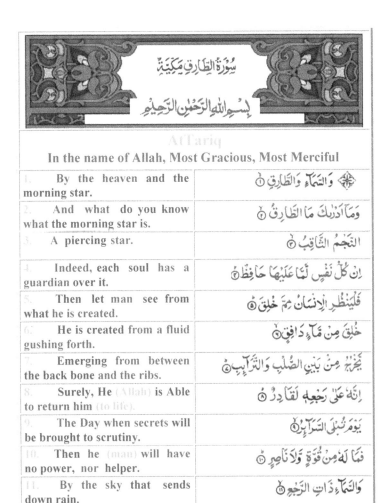

سُوْرَةُ الطَّارِقِ مَكِّيَّةٌ

بِسْمِ اللهِ الرَّحْمٰنِ الرَّحِيْمِ

In the name of Allah, Most Gracious, Most Merciful

1. By the heaven and the morning star.	وَالسَّمَاءِ وَالطَّارِقِ ۝
2. And what do you know what the morning star is.	وَمَآ اَدْرٰىكَ مَا الطَّارِقُ ۝
3. A piercing star.	النَّجْمُ الثَّاقِبُ ۝
4. Indeed, each soul has a guardian over it.	اِنْ كُلُّ نَفْسٍ لَّمَّا عَلَيْهَا حَافِظٌ ۝
5. Then let man see from what he is created.	فَلْيَنْظُرِ الْاِنْسَانُ مِمَّ خُلِقَ ۝
6. He is created from a fluid gushing forth.	خُلِقَ مِنْ مَّاءٍ دَافِقٍ ۝
7. Emerging from between the back bone and the ribs.	يَخْرُجُ مِنْ بَيْنِ الصُّلْبِ وَالتَّرَآئِبِ ۝
8. Surely, He (Allah) is Able to return him (to life).	اِنَّهُ عَلٰى رَجْعِهِ لَقَادِرٌ ۝
9. The Day when secrets will be brought to scrutiny.	يَوْمَ تُبْلَى السَّرَآئِرُ ۝
10. Then he (man) will have no power, nor helper.	فَمَا لَهُ مِنْ قُوَّةٍ وَّلَا نَاصِرٍ ۝
11. By the sky that sends down rain.	وَالسَّمَاءِ ذَاتِ الرَّجْعِ ۝

12. And the earth that splits (at the sprouting of vegetation).	وَالۡاَرۡضِ ذَاتِ الصَّدۡعِ ۙ ۝
13. Indeed, it (the Quran) is a decisive Word.	اِنَّهٗ لَقَوۡلٌ فَصۡلٌ ۙ ۝
14. And it is no amusement.	وَّمَا هُوَ بِالۡهَزۡلِ ؕ ۝
15. Indeed, they are plotting a plot.	اِنَّهُمۡ يَكِيۡدُوۡنَ كَيۡدًا ۙ ۝
16. And I am devising a plan.	وَّاَكِيۡدُ كَيۡدًا ۚ ۝
17. So give a respite to the disbelievers, leave them to themselves for a while.	فَمَهِّلِ الۡكٰفِرِيۡنَ اَمۡهِلۡهُمۡ رُوَيۡدًا ۝

AlAala

In the name of Allah, Most Gracious, Most Merciful

1. Glorify the name of your Lord, the Most High.	سَبِّحِ اسْمَ رَبِّكَ الْأَعْلَى ١
2. He Who created and proportioned.	الَّذِيْ خَلَقَ فَسَوّٰى ٢
3. And He Who set a destiny and guided.	وَالَّذِيْ قَدَّرَ فَهَدٰى ٣
4. And He Who brings out the pasture.	وَالَّذِيْ أَخْرَجَ الْمَرْعٰى ٤
5. Then makes it dark stubble.	فَجَعَلَهُ غُثَاءً أَحْوٰى ٥
6. We shall make you to recite, then you shall not forget.	سَنُقْرِئُكَ فَلَا تَنْسٰى ٦
7. Except what Allah wills. Surely, He knows (what is) apparent and what is hidden.	إِلَّا مَا شَاءَ اللهُ إِنَّهُ يَعْلَمُ الْجَهْرَ وَمَا يَخْفٰى ٧
8. And We shall make easy for you the easy way.	وَنُيَسِّرُكَ لِلْيُسْرٰى ٨
9. So remind (them), if the reminder should benefit.	فَذَكِّرْ إِنْ نَفَعَتِ الذِّكْرٰى ٩
10. The reminder will be received by him who fears.	سَيَذَّكَّرُ مَنْ يَخْشٰى ١٠

11. And it will be avoided by the wretched.	وَيَتَجَنَّبُهَا الْأَشْقَى ۝
12. He who shall (enter to) burn in the Great Fire.	الَّذِى يَصْلَى النَّارَ الْكُبْرَى ۝
13. Then neither dying therein, nor living.	ثُمَّ لَا يَمُوتُ فِيهَا وَلَا يَحْيَى ۝
14. Truly successful is he who purified himself.	قَدْ أَفْلَحَ مَنْ تَزَكَّى ۝
15. And remembered the name of his Lord, then prayed.	وَذَكَرَ اسْمَ رَبِّهِ فَصَلَّى ۝
16. But you prefer the life of this world.	بَلْ تُؤْثِرُونَ الْحَيَوةَ الدُّنْيَا ۝
17. Although the Hereafter is better and more lasting.	وَالْآخِرَةُ خَيْرٌ وَأَبْقَى ۝
18. Indeed, this is in the former scriptures.	إِنَّ هَذَا لَفِي الصُّحُفِ الْأُولَى ۝
19. The scriptures of Abraham and Moses.	صُحُفِ إِبْرَاهِيمَ وَمُوسَى ۝

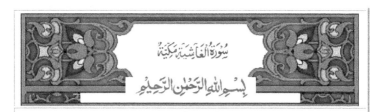

سُوْرَةُ الْغَاشِيَةِ مَكِّيَّةٌ

بِسْمِ اللهِ الرَّحْمٰنِ الرَّحِيْمِ

AlGhashia

In the name of Allah, Most Gracious, Most Merciful

1. Has there reached you the news of the overwhelming.	هَلْ اَتٰىكَ حَدِيْثُ الْغَاشِيَةِ ۞
2. (Some) faces on that Day shall be downcast.	وُجُوْهٌ يَّوْمَئِذٍ خَاشِعَةٌ ۞
3. Laboring, weary.	عَامِلَةٌ نَّاصِبَةٌ ۞
4. They will (enter to) burn in the hot blazing Fire.	تَصْلٰى نَارًا حَامِيَةً ۞
5. They will be given to drink from a boiling fountain.	تُسْقٰى مِنْ عَيْنٍ اٰنِيَةٍ ۞
6. No food for them except thorny dry grass.	لَيْسَ لَهُمْ طَعَامٌ اِلَّا مِنْ ضَرِيْعٍ ۞
7. Which will neither nourish nor satisfy hunger.	لَّا يُسْمِنُ وَلَا يُغْنِيْ مِنْ جُوْعٍ ۞
8. (Other) faces on that Day shall be joyful.	وُجُوْهٌ يَّوْمَئِذٍ نَّاعِمَةٌ ۞
9. With their efforts, well pleased.	لِّسَعْيِهَا رَاضِيَةٌ ۞
10. In elevated Garden.	فِيْ جَنَّةٍ عَالِيَةٍ ۞
11. They shall not hear therein idle talk.	لَّا تَسْمَعُ فِيْهَا لَاغِيَةً ۞

12. In it will be running spring.	فِيهَا عَيْنٌ جَارِيَةٌ ۞
13. In it there will be raised couches.	فِيهَا سُرُرٌ مَّرْفُوعَةٌ ۞
14. And goblets set in place.	وَّأَكْوَابٌ مَّوْضُوعَةٌ ۞
15. And cushions ranged in rows.	وَّنَمَارِقُ مَصْفُوفَةٌ ۞
16. And fine carpets spread out.	وَّزَرَابِيُّ مَبْثُوثَةٌ ۞
17. Then do they not look at the camels, how they are created.	أَفَلَا يَنْظُرُونَ إِلَى الْإِبِلِ كَيْفَ خُلِقَتْ ۞
18. And at the sky, how it is raised high.	وَإِلَى السَّمَاءِ كَيْفَ رُفِعَتْ ۞
19. And at the mountains, how they are firmly set.	وَإِلَى الْجِبَالِ كَيْفَ نُصِبَتْ ۞
20. And at the earth, how it is spread out.	وَإِلَى الْأَرْضِ كَيْفَ سُطِحَتْ ۞
21. So remind (O Muhammad), you are only an admonisher.	فَذَكِّرْ إِنَّمَا أَنْتَ مُذَكِّرٌ ۞
22. You are not over them a controller.	لَسْتَ عَلَيْهِمْ بِمُصَيْطِرٍ ۞
23. But him who turns away and disbelieves.	إِلَّا مَنْ تَوَلَّى وَكَفَرَ ۞
24. Then Allah will punish him with the greatest punishment.	فَيُعَذِّبُهُ اللَّهُ الْعَذَابَ الْأَكْبَرَ ۞
25. Indeed, to Us is their return.	إِنَّ إِلَيْنَا إِيَابَهُمْ ۞
26. Then indeed, upon Us is their account.	ثُمَّ إِنَّ عَلَيْنَا حِسَابَهُمْ ۞

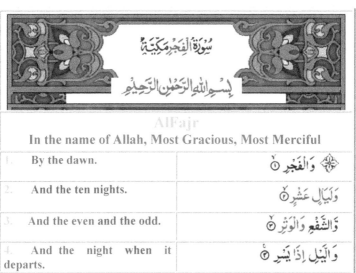

سُوْرَةُ الْفَجْرِ مَكِّيَّةٌ

بِسْمِ اللهِ الرَّحْمٰنِ الرَّحِيْمِ

In the name of Allah, Most Gracious, Most Merciful

1.	By the dawn.	۞ وَالْفَجْرِ ۝
2.	And the ten nights.	وَلَيَالٍ عَشْرٍ ۝
3.	And the even and the odd.	وَّالشَّفْعِ وَالْوَتْرِ ۝
4.	And the night when it departs.	وَالَّيْلِ اِذَا يَسْرِ ۝
5.	Is there in that an oath for one with sense.	هَلْ فِيْ ذٰلِكَ قَسَمٌ لِّذِيْ حِجْرٍ ۝
6.	Have you not considered how your Lord dealt with Aad.	اَلَمْ تَرَ كَيْفَ فَعَلَ رَبُّكَ بِعَادٍ ۝
7.	Iram of lofty pillars.	اِرَمَ ذَاتِ الْعِمَادِ ۝
8.	The like of whom had never been created in the lands.	الَّتِيْ لَمْ يُخْلَقْ مِثْلُهَا فِي الْبِلَادِ ۝
9.	And Thamud who had carved out the rocks in the valley.	وَثَمُوْدَ الَّذِيْنَ جَابُوا الصَّخْرَ بِالْوَادِ ۝
10.	And Pharaoh of the stakes.	وَفِرْعَوْنَ ذِى الْاَوْتَادِ ۝

11. (All), who did transgress beyond bounds in the lands.	الَّذِيۡنَ طَغَوۡا فِى الۡبِلَادِ ۖ
12. And spread much corruption in them.	فَاَكۡثَرُوۡا فِيۡهَا الۡفَسَادَ ۖ
13. So your Lord poured on them a scourge of punishment.	فَصَبَّ عَلَيۡهِمۡ رَبُّكَ سَوۡطَ عَذَابٍ ۖ
14. Indeed, your Lord is ever watchful (in ambush).	اِنَّ رَبَّكَ لَبِالۡمِرۡصَادِ ۖ
15. And as for man, when his Lord tries him, so He honors him and blesses him, then he says: "My Lord has honored me."	فَاَمَّا الۡاِنۡسَانُ اِذَا مَا ابۡتَلٰٮهُ رَبُّهٗ فَاَكۡرَمَهٗ وَنَعَّمَهٗ فَيَقُوۡلُ رَبِّىۡۤ اَكۡرَمَنِ ۖ
16. But when He tries him and restricts his provisions for him, then he says: "My Lord has humiliated me."	وَاَمَّاۤ اِذَا مَا ابۡتَلٰٮهُ فَقَدَرَ عَلَيۡهِ رِزۡقَهٗ فَيَقُوۡلُ رَبِّىۡۤ اَهَانَنِ ۖ
17. Nay, but you do not honor the orphan.	كَلَّا بَلۡ لَّا تُكۡرِمُوۡنَ الۡيَتِيۡمَ ۖ
18. And you do not encourage the feeding of needy.	وَلَا تَحٰٓضُّوۡنَ عَلٰى طَعَامِ الۡمِسۡكِيۡنِ ۖ
19. And you devour the inheritance devouring greedily.	وَتَاۡكُلُوۡنَ التُّرَاثَ اَكۡلًا لَّمًّا ۖ
20. And you love the wealth with immense love.	وَّتُحِبُّوۡنَ الۡمَالَ حُبًّا جَمًّا ۖ
21. Nay, when the earth is pounded to become a sand-desert.	كَلَّاۤ اِذَا دُكَّتِ الۡاَرۡضُ دَكًّا دَكًّا ۖ

22. And your Lord comes, and the angels (standing in) rank upon rank.	وَجَآءَ رَبُّكَ وَالْمَلَكُ صَفًّا صَفًّا ۞
23. And Hell on that Day is brought. That Day man shall remember, but what (good) to him will be the remembrance.	وَجِائَىَ يَوْمَئِذٍ بِجَهَنَّمَ ۚ يَوْمَئِذٍ يَّتَذَكَّرُ الْإِنْسَانُ وَأَنَّى لَهُ الذِّكْرَى ۞
24. He will say: "Would that I had provided in advance for this life of mine."	يَقُولُ يٰلَيْتَنِى قَدَّمْتُ لِحَيَاتِى ۞
25. Then on that Day, none can punish as His punishment.	فَيَوْمَئِذٍ لَّا يُعَذِّبُ عَذَابَهُ أَحَدٌ ۞
26. And none can bind as His binding.	وَلَا يُوثِقُ وَثَاقَهُ أَحَدٌ ۞
27. O peaceful and fully satisfied soul.	يَا أَيَّتُهَا النَّفْسُ الْمُطْمَئِنَّةُ ۞
28. Return to your Lord, well pleased, and well pleasing (in the sight of your Lord).	ارْجِعِى إِلَى رَبِّكِ رَاضِيَةً مَّرْضِيَّةً ۞
29. So enter among My servants.	فَادْخُلِى فِى عِبَادِى ۞
30. And enter My Paradise.	وَادْخُلِى جَنَّتِى ۞

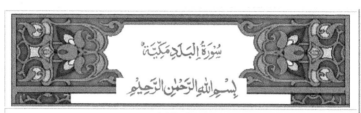

AlBalad

In the name of Allah, Most Gracious, Most Merciful

1. Nay, I swear by this city (Makkah).	لَآ أُقْسِمُ بِهَٰذَا الْبَلَدِ ۞
2. And you (O Muhammad) are free of restriction in this city.	وَأَنتَ حِلٌّ بِهَٰذَا الْبَلَدِ ۞
3. And (I swear by) the father and the children he begot.	وَوَالِدٍ وَمَا وَلَدَ ۞
4. We have indeed created man in hardship.	لَقَدْ خَلَقْنَا الْإِنسَانَ فِي كَبَدٍ ۞
5. Does he think that no one will have power over him.	أَيَحْسَبُ أَن لَّن يَقْدِرَ عَلَيْهِ أَحَدٌ ۞
6. He says, "I have squandered heaps of wealth."	يَقُولُ أَهْلَكْتُ مَالًا لُّبَدًا ۞
7. Does he think that no one has seen him.	أَيَحْسَبُ أَن لَّمْ يَرَهُ أَحَدٌ ۞
8. Have We not made for him two eyes.	أَلَمْ نَجْعَل لَّهُ عَيْنَيْنِ ۞
9. And a tongue and two lips.	وَلِسَانًا وَشَفَتَيْنِ ۞
10. And We have shown him the two ways (good and evil).	وَهَدَيْنَاهُ النَّجْدَيْنِ ۞
11. But he has not made effort through the steep pass.	فَلَا اقْتَحَمَ الْعَقَبَةَ ۞

12. And what do you know what the steep pass is.	وَمَآ أَدْرٰىكَ مَا الْعَقَبَةُ ۞
13. It is the freeing of a neck from bondage.	فَكُّ رَقَبَةٍ ۞
14. Or feeding on a day of severe hunger.	أَوْ اِطْعٰمٌ فِيْ يَوْمٍ ذِيْ مَسْغَبَةٍ ۞
15. An orphan nearly related.	يَّتِيْمًا ذَا مَقْرَبَةٍ ۞
16. Or a needy lying in the dust.	أَوْ مِسْكِيْنًا ذَا مَتْرَبَةٍ ۞
17. Then being among those who have believed, and advised one another to patience, and advised one another to mercy.	ثُمَّ كَانَ مِنَ الَّذِيْنَ اٰمَنُوْا وَتَوَاصَوْا بِالصَّبْرِ وَتَوَاصَوْا بِالْمَرْحَمَةِ ۞
18. Those are the people of the right hand.	أُولٰٓئِكَ أَصْحٰبُ الْمَيْمَنَةِ ۞
19. And those who disbelieved in Our revelations, they are the people of the left hand.	وَالَّذِيْنَ كَفَرُوْا بِاٰيٰتِنَا هُمْ أَصْحٰبُ الْمَشْئَمَةِ ۞
20. The Fire will be closed in over them.	عَلَيْهِمْ نَارٌ مُّوْصَدَةٌ ۞

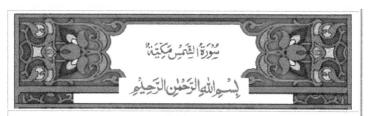

AshShams

In the name of Allah, Most Gracious, Most Merciful

1. By the sun and his brightness.	وَالشَّمْسِ وَضُحٰىهَا ۞
2. And the moon when it follows it (the sun).	وَالْقَمَرِ إِذَا تَلٰهَا ۞
3. And the day when it shows up its (sun's) brightness.	وَالنَّهَارِ إِذَا جَلّٰهَا ۞
4. And the night when it covers it up (the sun).	وَالَّيْلِ إِذَا يَغْشٰهَا ۞
5. And the heaven and Him Who built it.	وَالسَّمَآءِ وَمَا بَنٰهَا ۞
6. And the earth and Him Who spread it.	وَالْاَرْضِ وَمَا طَحٰهَا ۞
7. And the human soul and Him Who proportioned it.	وَنَفْسٍ وَّمَا سَوّٰهَا ۞
8. Then inspired it with its wickedness and its righteousness.	فَاَلْهَمَهَا فُجُوْرَهَا وَتَقْوٰىهَا ۞
9. Truly successful is he who purified it.	قَدْ اَفْلَحَ مَنْ زَكّٰىهَا ۞
10. And truly a failure is he who corrupted it.	وَقَدْ خَابَ مَنْ دَسّٰهَا ۞

11.　Thamud denied because of their transgression.	كَذَّبَتْ ثَمُوْدُ بِطَغْوٰىهَا ۞
12.　When the most wretched of them was sent forth.	اِذِ انْبَعَثَ اَشْقٰىهَا ۞
13.　So the Messenger of Allah said to them, "(It is) the she camel of Allah so let her drink."	فَقَالَ لَهُمْ رَسُوْلُ اللّٰهِ نَاقَةَ اللّٰهِ وَسُقْيٰهَا ۞
14.　Then they denied him, and they hamstrung her, so their Lord let loose a scourge upon them for their sin, and leveled them down (all together in destruction).	فَكَذَّبُوْهُ فَعَقَرُوْهَا ۙ فَدَمْدَمَ عَلَيْهِمْ رَبُّهُمْ بِذَنْۢبِهِمْ فَسَوّٰىهَا ۞
15.　And He (Allah) feared not the consequences thereof.	وَلَا يَخَافُ عُقْبٰهَا ۞

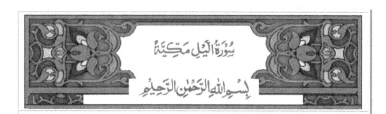

In the name of Allah, Most Gracious, Most Merciful

1. By the night when it covers.	وَالَّيۡلِ اِذَا يَغۡشٰى ۞
2. And the day when it appears in brightness.	وَالنَّهَارِ اِذَا تَجَلّٰى ۞
3. And Him Who created the male and the female.	وَمَا خَلَقَ الذَّكَرَ وَالۡاُنۡثٰىۤ ۞
4. Indeed, your efforts are diverse.	اِنَّ سَعۡيَكُمۡ لَشَتّٰى ۞
5. So he who gives (in charity) and fears (Allah).	فَاَمَّا مَنۡ اَعۡطٰى وَاتَّقٰى ۞
6. And believes in goodness.	وَصَدَّقَ بِالۡحُسۡنٰى ۞
7. So We shall make smooth for him the path of ease.	فَسَنُيَسِّرُهٗ لِلۡيُسۡرٰى ۞
8. And he who is miser, and thinks himself as self sufficient.	وَاَمَّا مَنۡ بَخِلَ وَاسۡتَغۡنٰى ۞
9. And belies to goodness.	وَكَذَّبَ بِالۡحُسۡنٰى ۞
10. So We shall make smooth for him the path of difficulty.	فَسَنُيَسِّرُهٗ لِلۡعُسۡرٰى ۞
11. And what will avail him his wealth when he perishes.	وَمَا يُغۡنِىۡ عَنۡهُ مَالُهٗۤ اِذَا تَرَدّٰى ۞

12. Indeed, it is for Us (to give) guidance.	اِنَّ عَلَيْنَا لَلْهُدٰى ۞
13. And indeed, Ours are the Hereafter and this present life.	وَاِنَّ لَنَا لَلْاٰخِرَةَ وَالْاُوْلٰى ۞
14. So, I have warned you of the blazing Fire.	فَاَنْذَرْتُكُمْ نَارًا تَلَظّٰى ۞
15. None shall (enter to) burn in it except the most wretched.	لَا يَصْلٰىهَآ اِلَّا الْاَشْقَى ۞
16. He who belied and turned away.	الَّذِىْ كَذَّبَ وَتَوَلّٰى ۞
17. And away from it shall be kept the righteous.	وَسَيُجَنَّبُهَا الْاَتْقَى ۞
18. He who gives his wealth to purify (himself).	الَّذِىْ يُؤْتِىْ مَالَهٗ يَتَزَكّٰى ۞
19. And not (giving) for anyone who has (done him) a favor to be rewarded.	وَمَا لِاَحَدٍ عِنْدَهٗ مِنْ نِعْمَةٍ تُجْزٰى ۞
20. Except as seeking the goodwill of his Lord, the Exalted.	اِلَّا ابْتِغَآءَ وَجْهِ رَبِّهِ الْاَعْلٰى ۞
21. And He will certainly be well pleased.	وَلَسَوْفَ يَرْضٰى ۞

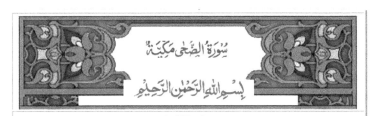

In the name of Allah, Most Gracious, Most Merciful

1.	By the morning brightness.	وَالضُّحَىٰ ۝
2.	And the night when it covers with darkness.	وَالَّيْلِ إِذَا سَجَىٰ ۝
3.	Your Lord has not forsaken you, nor is He displeased.	مَا وَدَّعَكَ رَبُّكَ وَمَا قَلَىٰ ۝
4.	And indeed the Hereafter is better for you than the present (life of this world).	وَلَلْآخِرَةُ خَيْرٌ لَّكَ مِنَ الْأُولَىٰ ۝
5.	And your Lord shall soon give you (much), so you shall be well pleased.	وَلَسَوْفَ يُعْطِيكَ رَبُّكَ فَتَرْضَىٰ ۝
6.	Did He not find you an orphan, then He sheltered you.	أَلَمْ يَجِدْكَ يَتِيمًا فَآوَىٰ ۝
7.	And He found you lost of the Way, then He guided (you).	وَوَجَدَكَ ضَالًّا فَهَدَىٰ ۝
8.	And He found you poor, then He enriched you.	وَوَجَدَكَ عَآئِلًا فَأَغْنَىٰ ۝
9.	So as for the orphan, do not be harsh.	فَأَمَّا الْيَتِيمَ فَلَا تَقْهَرْ ۝

10. And as for the beggar, do not repel.	وَأَمَّا السَّآئِلَ فَلَا تَنْهَرْ ۝
11. And as for the bounty of your lord, do proclaim.	وَأَمَّا بِنِعْمَةِ رَبِّكَ فَحَدِّثْ ۝

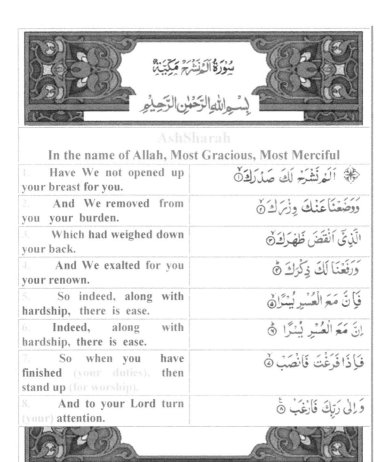

سُوْرَةُ الْاِنْشِرَاحُ مَكِّيَّةٌ

بِسْمِ اللهِ الرَّحْمٰنِ الرَّحِيْمِ

In the name of Allah, Most Gracious, Most Merciful

1.	Have We not opened up your breast for you.	اَلَمْ نَشْرَحْ لَكَ صَدْرَكَۙ ۱
2.	And We removed from you your burden.	وَوَضَعْنَا عَنْكَ وِزْرَكَۙ ۲
3.	Which had weighed down your back.	الَّذِيْٓ اَنْقَضَ ظَهْرَكَۙ ۳
4.	And We exalted for you your renown.	وَرَفَعْنَا لَكَ ذِكْرَكَؕ ۴
5.	So indeed, along with hardship, there is ease.	فَاِنَّ مَعَ الْعُسْرِ يُسْرًاۙ ۵
6.	Indeed, along with hardship, there is ease.	اِنَّ مَعَ الْعُسْرِ يُسْرًاؕ ۶
7.	So when you have finished (your duties), then stand up (for worship).	فَاِذَا فَرَغْتَ فَانْصَبْۙ ۷
8.	And to your Lord turn (your) attention.	وَاِلٰى رَبِّكَ فَارْغَبْؒ ۸

سُوْرَةُ التِّيْنِ مَكِّيَةٌ

بِسْمِ اللهِ الرَّحْمٰنِ الرَّحِيْمِ

In the name of Allah, Most Gracious, Most Merciful

1.	By the fig and the olive.	۝ وَالتِّيْنِ وَالزَّيْتُوْنِ ۝
2.	And the Mount Sinai.	وَطُوْرِ سِيْنِيْنَ ۝
3.	And this city of security (Makkah).	وَهٰذَا الْبَلَدِ الْاَمِيْنِ ۝
4.	We have certainly created man in the finest of moulds.	لَقَدْ خَلَقْنَا الْاِنْسَانَ فِيْٓ اَحْسَنِ تَقْوِيْمٍ ۝
5.	Then We reversed him to the lowest of the low.	ثُمَّ رَدَدْنٰهُ اَسْفَلَ سٰفِلِيْنَ ۝
6.	Except those who believe and do righteous deeds. For them is a reward without end.	اِلَّا الَّذِيْنَ اٰمَنُوْا وَعَمِلُوا الصّٰلِحٰتِ فَلَهُمْ اَجْرٌ غَيْرُ مَمْنُوْنٍ ۝
7.	Then what can deny you, after this, as to the judgment.	فَمَا يُكَذِّبُكَ بَعْدُ بِالدِّيْنِ ۝
8.	Is not Allah the most just of judges.	اَلَيْسَ اللهُ بِاَحْكَمِ الْحٰكِمِيْنَ ۝

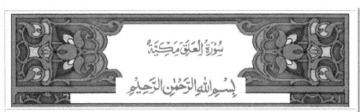

AlAlaq

In the name of Allah, Most Gracious, Most Merciful

1. Read in the name of your Lord Who created.	اقْرَأْ بِاسْمِ رَبِّكَ الَّذِي خَلَقَ ۞
2. Created man from a clot of congealed blood.	خَلَقَ الْإِنْسَانَ مِنْ عَلَقٍ ۞
3. Read and your Lord is Most Generous.	اقْرَأْ وَرَبُّكَ الْأَكْرَمُ ۞
4. Who taught (knowledge) by the pen.	الَّذِي عَلَّمَ بِالْقَلَمِ ۞
5. Taught man that which he did not know.	عَلَّمَ الْإِنْسَانَ مَا لَمْ يَعْلَمْ ۞
6. Nay, indeed, man transgress rebelliously.	كَلَّا إِنَّ الْإِنْسَانَ لَيَطْغَى ۞
7. Because he sees (himself) self sufficient.	أَنْ رَآهُ اسْتَغْنَى ۞
8. Indeed, to your Lord is the return.	إِنَّ إِلَى رَبِّكَ الرُّجْعَى ۞
9. Have you seen the one who forbids.	أَرَأَيْتَ الَّذِي يَنْهَى ۞
10. A servant when he prays.	عَبْدًا إِذَا صَلَّى ۞
11. Have you seen, if he (the servant) be upon guidance.	أَرَأَيْتَ إِنْ كَانَ عَلَى الْهُدَى ۞

12. Or enjoins righteousness.	اَوۡ اَمَرَ بِالتَّقۡوٰی ۞
13. Have you seen, if he denies and turns away.	اَرَءَیۡتَ اِنۡ کَذَّبَ وَتَوَلّٰی ۞
14. Does he not know that Allah sees.	اَلَمۡ یَعۡلَمۡ بِاَنَّ اللهَ یَرٰی ۞
15. Nay, if he does not desist, We shall surely drag him by his forelock.	کَلَّا لَئِنۡ لَّمۡ یَنۡتَهِ ۬ لَنَسۡفَعًۢا بِالنَّاصِیَةِ ۞
16. The forelock, lying and sinful.	نَاصِیَةٍ کَاذِبَةٍ خَاطِئَةٍ ۞
17. So let him call his supporters.	فَلۡیَدۡعُ نَادِیَهٗ ۞
18. We shall call the angels of torment.	سَنَدۡعُ الزَّبَانِیَةَ ۞
19. Nay, do not obey him, and prostrate, and draw closer (to Allah). *AsSajda*	کَلَّا ۭ لَا تُطِعۡهُ وَاسۡجُدۡ وَاقۡتَرِبۡ ۩ ۞

سُورَةُ الْقَدْرِ مَكِّيَّةٌ

بِسْمِ اللهِ الرَّحْمٰنِ الرَّحِيْمِ

AlQadar

In the name of Allah, Most Gracious, Most Merciful

1. Indeed, We sent it down (the Quran) in the Night of Power.	اِنَّآ اَنْزَلْنٰهُ فِيْ لَيْلَةِ الْقَدْرِ ۚ
2. And what do you know what the Night of Power is.	وَمَآ اَدْرٰىكَ مَا لَيْلَةُ الْقَدْرِ ۚ
3. The Night of Power is better than a thousand months.	لَيْلَةُ الْقَدْرِ ۙ خَيْرٌ مِّنْ اَلْفِ شَهْرٍ ۚ
4. The angels and the Spirit descend in it, by the permission of their Lord with every decree.	تَنَزَّلُ الْمَلٰٓئِكَةُ وَالرُّوْحُ فِيْهَا بِاِذْنِ رَبِّهِمْ ۚ مِّنْ كُلِّ اَمْرٍ ۚ
5. Peace is that (night), until the appearance of the dawn.	سَلٰمٌ ۛ هِيَ حَتّٰى مَطْلَعِ الْفَجْرِ ۚ

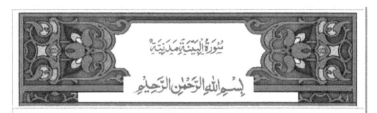

AlBayyana

In the name of Allah, Most Gracious, Most Merciful

1. Those who disbelieve among the People of the Scripture, and those who associate (with Allah) would not desist until there comes to them clear evidence.	لَمْ يَكُنِ الَّذِينَ كَفَرُوا مِنْ اَهْلِ الْكِتَبِ وَالْمُشْرِكِينَ مُنْفَكِّينَ حَتَّى تَأْتِيَهُمُ الْبَيِّنَةُ ۞
2. A Messenger from Allah, reciting purified pages (of Scripture).	رَسُولٌ مِّنَ اللهِ يَتْلُوا صُحُفًا مُّطَهَّرَةً ۞
3. Within it are writings (decrees), straight.	فِيهَا كُتُبٌ قَيِّمَةٌ ۞
4. Nor did those who were given the Scripture (before this) divide until after what had come to them as clear evidence.	وَمَا تَفَرَّقَ الَّذِينَ أُوتُوا الْكِتَبَ اِلَّا مِنْ بَعْدِ مَا جَآءَتْهُمُ الْبَيِّنَةُ ۞
5. And they were not commanded except to worship Allah, (being) sincere to Him in religion, true (in faith), and to establish the prayer, and to give the poor-due. And that is the true (and right) religion.	وَمَا أُمِرُوا اِلَّا لِيَعْبُدُوا اللهَ مُخْلِصِينَ لَهُ الدِّينَ ۛ حُنَفَآءَ وَيُقِيمُوا الصَّلوةَ وَيُؤْتُوا الزَّكوةَ وَذَلِكَ دِينُ الْقَيِّمَةِ ۞

6. Indeed, those who disbelieved among the People of the Scripture, and those who associated (with Allah) shall be in the fire of Hell, abiding therein for ever. Those are the worst of creatures.	اِنَّ الَّذِيْنَ كَفَرُوْا مِنْ اَهْلِ الْكِتٰبِ وَالْمُشْرِكِيْنَ فِيْ نَارِ جَهَنَّمَ خٰلِدِيْنَ فِيْهَا ؕ اُولٰٓئِكَ هُمْ شَرُّ الْبَرِيَّةِ ۝
7. Indeed, those who believed and did righteous deeds, those are the best of creatures.	اِنَّ الَّذِيْنَ اٰمَنُوْا وَعَمِلُوا الصّٰلِحٰتِ اُولٰٓئِكَ هُمْ خَيْرُ الْبَرِيَّةِ ۝
8. Their reward with their Lord shall be Gardens of Eternity beneath which rivers flow, they shall abide therein forever. Allah being pleased with them and they being pleased with Him. That is for him who feared his Lord.	جَزَآؤُهُمْ عِنْدَ رَبِّهِمْ جَنّٰتُ عَدْنٍ تَجْرِيْ مِنْ تَحْتِهَا الْاَنْهٰرُ خٰلِدِيْنَ فِيْهَا اَبَدًا ؕ رَضِيَ اللّٰهُ عَنْهُمْ وَرَضُوْا عَنْهُ ؕ ذٰلِكَ لِمَنْ خَشِيَ رَبَّهٗ ۝

In the name of Allah, Most Gracious, Most Merciful

1. When the earth is shaken with its (utmost) earthquake.	۞ اِذَا زُلْزِلَتِ الْاَرْضُ زِلْزَالَهَا ۞
2. And the earth throws out its burdens.	وَاَخْرَجَتِ الْاَرْضُ اَثْقَالَهَا ۞
3. And man says: "What is (the matter) with it."	وَقَالَ الْاِنْسَانُ مَالَهَا ۞
4. That Day it will report its news.	يَوْمَئِذٍ تُحَدِّثُ اَخْبَارَهَا ۞
5. Because your Lord has inspired (commanded) it.	بِاَنَّ رَبَّكَ اَوْحٰى لَهَا ۞
6. That day mankind shall proceed in scattered groups, to be shown their deeds.	يَوْمَئِذٍ يَّصْدُرُ النَّاسُ اَشْتَاتًا ۙ لِيُرَوْا اَعْمَالَهُمْ ۞
7. So whoever does an atom's weight of good, shall see it.	فَمَنْ يَّعْمَلْ مِثْقَالَ ذَرَّةٍ خَيْرًا يَّرَهُ ۞
8. And whoever does an atom's weight of evil, shall see it.	وَمَنْ يَّعْمَلْ مِثْقَالَ ذَرَّةٍ شَرًّا يَّرَهُ ۞

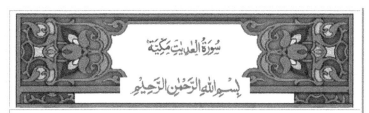

AlAdiat

In the name of Allah, Most Gracious, Most Merciful

1. By the (horses) who run with panting (breath).	وَالْعٰدِيٰتِ ضَبْحًا ۞
2. Then strike sparks (with their hoofs).	فَالْمُوْرِيٰتِ قَدْحًا ۞
3. Then charge suddenly in the morning.	فَالْمُغِيْرٰتِ صُبْحًا ۞
4. Then raise up thereby (clouds of) dust.	فَاَثَرْنَ بِهٖ نَقْعًا ۞
5. Then penetrate thereby into the midst (of enemy) collectively.	فَوَسَطْنَ بِهٖ جَمْعًا ۞
6. Indeed, mankind is ungrateful to his Lord.	اِنَّ الْاِنْسَانَ لِرَبِّهٖ لَكَنُوْدٌ ۞
7. And indeed, he himself is a witness to that.	وَاِنَّهٗ عَلٰى ذٰلِكَ لَشَهِيْدٌ ۞
8. And indeed, for the love of the worldly wealth, he is intense.	وَاِنَّهٗ لِحُبِّ الْخَيْرِ لَشَدِيْدٌ ۞
9. Does he not know, when that which is in the graves shall be brought out.	اَفَلَا يَعْلَمُ اِذَا بُعْثِرَ مَا فِى الْقُبُوْرِ ۞
10. And that which is in the breasts shall be made manifest.	وَحُصِّلَ مَا فِى الصُّدُوْرِ ۞

11. Indeed, their Lord on that Day shall be well informed of them.

إِنَّ رَبَّهُم بِهِمْ يَوْمَئِذٍ لَّخَبِيرٌ ۝

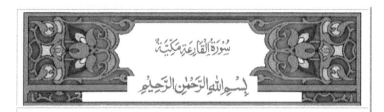

AlQaria

In the name of Allah, Most Gracious, Most Merciful

1. The striking calamity.	۞ اَلْقَارِعَةُ ۝
2. What is the striking calamity.	مَا الْقَارِعَةُ ۝
3. And what do you know what is the striking calamity.	وَمَآ اَدْرٰىكَ مَا الْقَارِعَةُ ۝
4. The Day when people shall be like scattered moths.	يَوْمَ يَكُوْنُ النَّاسُ كَالْفَرَاشِ الْمَبْثُوْثِ ۝
5. And the mountains shall be like carded wool.	وَتَكُوْنُ الْجِبَالُ كَالْعِهْنِ الْمَنْفُوْشِ ۝
6. Then he whose scales are heavy.	فَاَمَّا مَنْ ثَقُلَتْ مَوَازِيْنُهُ ۝
7. So he shall be in a state of pleasure.	فَهُوَ فِيْ عِيْشَةٍ رَّاضِيَةٍ ۝
8. And he whose scales are light.	وَاَمَّا مَنْ خَفَّتْ مَوَازِيْنُهُ ۝
9. So his refuge shall be the deep pit (of Hell).	فَاُمُّهُ هَاوِيَةٌ ۝
10. And what do you know what that is.	وَمَآ اَدْرٰىكَ مَا هِيَهْ ۝
11. A raging Fire.	نَارٌ حَامِيَةٌ ۝

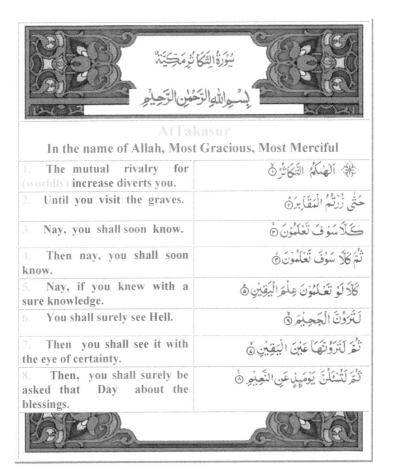

سُوْرَةُ التَّكَاثُرُ مَكِّيَّةٌ

بِسْمِ اللهِ الرَّحْمٰنِ الرَّحِيْمِ

At Takasur

In the name of Allah, Most Gracious, Most Merciful

1. The mutual rivalry for (worldly) increase diverts you.	اَلْهٰىكُمُ التَّكَاثُرُۙ ﴿١﴾
2. Until you visit the graves.	حَتّٰى زُرْتُمُ الْمَقَابِرَؕ ﴿٢﴾
3. Nay, you shall soon know.	كَلَّا سَوْفَ تَعْلَمُوْنَۙ ﴿٣﴾
4. Then nay, you shall soon know.	ثُمَّ كَلَّا سَوْفَ تَعْلَمُوْنَ ﴿٤﴾
5. Nay, if you knew with a sure knowledge.	كَلَّا لَوْ تَعْلَمُوْنَ عِلْمَ الْيَقِيْنِؕ ﴿٥﴾
6. You shall surely see Hell.	لَتَرَوُنَّ الْجَحِيْمَۙ ﴿٦﴾
7. Then you shall see it with the eye of certainty.	ثُمَّ لَتَرَوُنَّهَا عَيْنَ الْيَقِيْنِۙ ﴿٧﴾
8. Then, you shall surely be asked that Day about the blessings.	ثُمَّ لَتُسْـَٔلُنَّ يَوْمَئِذٍ عَنِ النَّعِيْمِ ﴿٨﴾

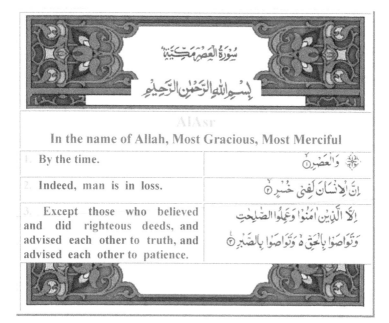

سُوْرَةُ الْعَصْرِ مَكِّيَّةٌ

بِسْمِ اللهِ الرَّحْمٰنِ الرَّحِيْمِ

In the name of Allah, Most Gracious, Most Merciful

1. By the time.	وَالْعَصْرِۙ ۞ ①
2. Indeed, man is in loss.	إِنَّ الْاِنْسَانَ لَفِيْ خُسْرٍۙ ②
3. Except those who believed and did righteous deeds, and advised each other to truth, and advised each other to patience.	اِلَّا الَّذِيْنَ اٰمَنُوْا وَعَمِلُوا الصّٰلِحٰتِ وَتَوَاصَوْا بِالْحَقِّ ۙ ة وَتَوَاصَوْا بِالصَّبْرِ ③

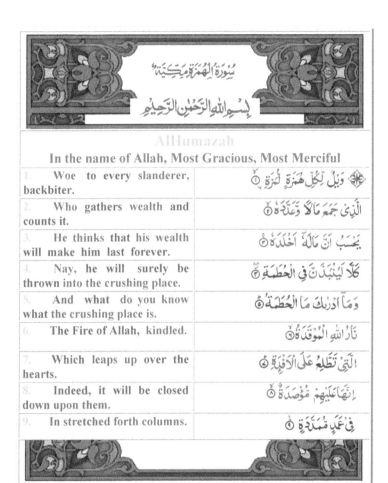

سُوْرَةُ الْهُمَزَةِ مَكِّيَّةٌ

بِسْمِ اللهِ الرَّحْمٰنِ الرَّحِيْمِ

AlHumazah

In the name of Allah, Most Gracious, Most Merciful

1.	Woe to every slanderer, backbiter.	وَيْلٌ لِّكُلِّ هُمَزَةٍ لُّمَزَةٍ ۞
2.	Who gathers wealth and counts it.	الَّذِيْ جَمَعَ مَالًا وَّعَدَّدَهٗ ۞
3.	He thinks that his wealth will make him last forever.	يَحْسَبُ اَنَّ مَالَهٗٓ اَخْلَدَهٗ ۞
4.	Nay, he will surely be thrown into the crushing place.	كَلَّا لَيُنْبَذَنَّ فِي الْحُطَمَةِ ۞
5.	And what do you know what the crushing place is.	وَمَآ اَدْرٰىكَ مَا الْحُطَمَةُ ۞
6.	The Fire of Allah, kindled.	نَارُ اللهِ الْمُوْقَدَةُ ۞
7.	Which leaps up over the hearts.	الَّتِيْ تَطَّلِعُ عَلَى الْاَفْئِدَةِ ۞
8.	Indeed, it will be closed down upon them.	اِنَّهَا عَلَيْهِمْ مُّؤْصَدَةٌ ۞
9.	In stretched forth columns.	فِيْ عَمَدٍ مُّمَدَّدَةٍ ۞

سُوْرَةُ الْفِيْلِ مَكِّيَّةٌ

بِسْمِ اللهِ الرَّحْمٰنِ الرَّحِيْمِ

In the name of Allah, Most Gracious, Most Merciful

1. Have you not considered how your Lord dealt with the people of the elephant.	اَلَمْ تَرَ كَيْفَ فَعَلَ رَبُّكَ بِاَصْحٰبِ الْفِيْلِ ۱
2. Did He not cause their plot to end in vain.	اَلَمْ يَجْعَلْ كَيْدَهُمْ فِيْ تَضْلِيْلٍ ۲
3. And He sent down on them birds in flocks.	وَاَرْسَلَ عَلَيْهِمْ طَيْرًا اَبَابِيْلَ ۳
4. Striking them with stones of baked clay.	تَرْمِيْهِمْ بِحِجَارَةٍ مِّنْ سِجِّيْلٍ ۴
5. Then He made them like straw eaten up (by cattle).	فَجَعَلَهُمْ كَعَصْفٍ مَّاْكُوْلٍ ۵

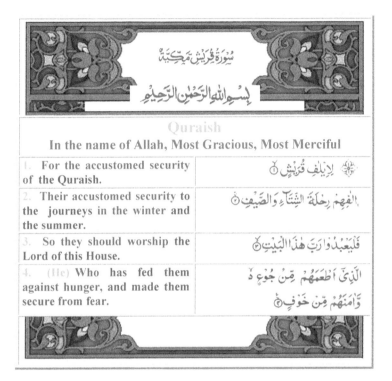

سُوْرَةُ قُرَيْشٍ مَكِّيَّةٌ

بِسْمِ اللهِ الرَّحْمٰنِ الرَّحِيْمِ

Quraish

In the name of Allah, Most Gracious, Most Merciful

1. For the accustomed security of the Quraish.	لِإِيْلٰفِ قُرَيْشٍ ۞
2. Their accustomed security to the journeys in the winter and the summer.	اٖلٰفِهِمْ رِحْلَةَ الشِّتَآءِ وَالصَّيْفِ ۞
3. So they should worship the Lord of this House.	فَلْيَعْبُدُوْا رَبَّ هٰذَا الْبَيْتِ ۞
4. (He) Who has fed them against hunger, and made them secure from fear.	الَّذِيْٓ أَطْعَمَهُمْ مِّنْ جُوْعٍ ۙ وَّاٰمَنَهُمْ مِّنْ خَوْفٍ ۞

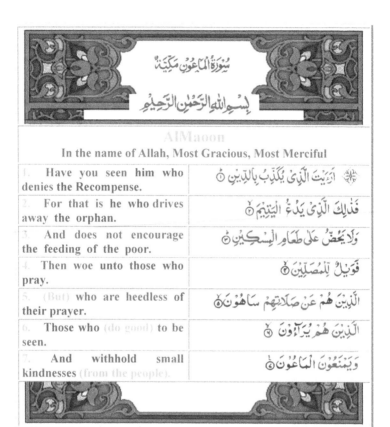

سُوْرَةُ الْمَاعُوْنِ مَكِّيَّةٌ	
بِسْمِ اللهِ الرَّحْمٰنِ الرَّحِيْمِ	

In the name of Allah, Most Gracious, Most Merciful

1. Have you seen him who denies the Recompense.	اَرَءَيْتَ الَّذِىْ يُكَذِّبُ بِالدِّيْنِ ۝
2. For that is he who drives away the orphan.	فَذٰلِكَ الَّذِىْ يَدُعُّ الْيَتِيْمَ ۝
3. And does not encourage the feeding of the poor.	وَلَا يَحُضُّ عَلٰى طَعَامِ الْمِسْكِيْنِ ۝
4. Then woe unto those who pray.	فَوَيْلٌ لِّلْمُصَلِّيْنَ ۝
5. (But) who are heedless of their prayer.	الَّذِيْنَ هُمْ عَنْ صَلَاتِهِمْ سَاهُوْنَ ۝
6. Those who (do good) to be seen.	الَّذِيْنَ هُمْ يُرَآءُوْنَ ۝
7. And withhold small kindnesses (from the people).	وَيَمْنَعُوْنَ الْمَاعُوْنَ ۝

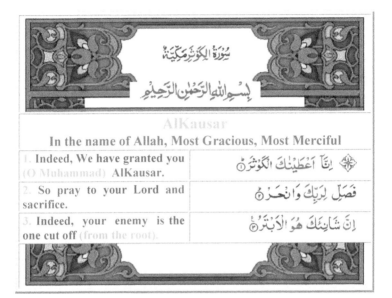

سُوْرَةُ الْكَوْثَرِ مَكِّيَّةٌ

بِسْمِ اللهِ الرَّحْمٰنِ الرَّحِيْمِ

AlKausar

In the name of Allah, Most Gracious, Most Merciful

1. Indeed, We have granted you (O Muhammad) AlKausar.	اِنَّآ اَعْطَيْنٰكَ الْكَوْثَرَ ۞
2. So pray to your Lord and sacrifice.	فَصَلِّ لِرَبِّكَ وَانْحَرْ ۞
3. Indeed, your enemy is the one cut off (from the root).	اِنَّ شَانِئَكَ هُوَ الْاَبْتَرُ ۞

سُورَةُ الكٰفِرُوۡنَ مَكِّيَّةٌ

بِسۡمِ اللّٰهِ الرَّحۡمٰنِ الرَّحِيۡمِ

In the name of Allah, Most Gracious, Most Merciful

1. Say, "O disbelievers."	قُلۡ يٰۤاَيُّهَا الۡكٰفِرُوۡنَ ۙ
2. "I do not worship that which you worship."	لَاۤ اَعۡبُدُ مَا تَعۡبُدُوۡنَ ۙ
3. "Nor are you worshippers of that which I worship."	وَلَاۤ اَنۡتُمۡ عٰبِدُوۡنَ مَاۤ اَعۡبُدُ ۚ
4. "Nor am I a worshipper of that which you worship."	وَلَاۤ اَنَا عَابِدٌ مَّا عَبَدۡتُّمۡ ۙ
5. "Nor are you worshippers of that which I worship."	وَلَاۤ اَنۡتُمۡ عٰبِدُوۡنَ مَاۤ اَعۡبُدُ ؕ
6. "For you is your religion, and for me is my religion."	لَكُمۡ دِيۡنُكُمۡ وَلِيَ دِيۡنِ ۟

سُوْرَةُ النَّصْرِ مَدَنِيَّةٌ

بِسْمِ اللهِ الرَّحْمٰنِ الرَّحِيْمِ

AlNasar

In the name of Allah, Most Gracious, Most Merciful

1. When Allah's help comes and victory (is attained).	١ اِذَا جَآءَ نَصْرُ اللهِ وَالْفَتْحُ ۙ
2. And you see the people entering into the religion of Allah in multitudes.	وَرَاَيْتَ النَّاسَ يَدْخُلُوْنَ فِيْ دِيْنِ اللهِ اَفْوَاجًا ۙ
3. Then glorify with praise of your Lord, and ask for His forgiveness. Indeed, He is ever accepting repentance.	فَسَبِّحْ بِحَمْدِ رَبِّكَ وَاسْتَغْفِرْهُ ۙ اِنَّهُ كَانَ تَوَّابًا ۙ

سُوْرَةُ اللَّهَبْ مَكِّيَّةٌ

بِسْمِ اللهِ الرَّحْمٰنِ الرَّحِيْمِ

Al-Lahab

In the name of Allah, Most Gracious, Most Merciful

1. May the hands of Abu Lahab be ruined, and ruined is he.	تَبَّتْ يَدَآ اَبِىْ لَهَبٍ وَّتَبَّ ۟
2. His wealth will not avail him and that which he earned.	مَآ اَغْنٰى عَنْهُ مَالُهُ وَمَا كَسَبَ ۟
3. He shall (enter to) burn into a blazing Fire.	سَيَصْلٰى نَارًا ذَاتَ لَهَبٍ ۟
4. And his wife, the carrier of slander (or wood thorns).	وَّامْرَاَتُهُ ۟ حَمَّالَةَ الْحَطَبِ ۟
5. Around her neck will be a rope of (twisted) palm-fiber.	فِىْ جِيْدِهَا حَبْلٌ مِّنْ مَّسَدٍ ۟

سُورَةُ الْاِخْلَاصِ مَكِّيَّةٌ

بِسْمِ اللهِ الرَّحْمٰنِ الرَّحِيمِ

Allkhlas

In the name of Allah, Most Gracious, Most Merciful

1.	Say: "He is Allah, the One."	۞ قُلْ هُوَ اللهُ اَحَدٌ ۞
2.	"Allah, the Self Sufficient."	اَللهُ الصَّمَدُ ۞
3.	"He begets not, nor was He begotten."	لَمْ يَلِدْ ۙ وَ لَمْ يُوْلَدْ ۞
4.	"And no one is equivalent with Him."	وَلَمْ يَكُنْ لَّهٗ كُفُوًا اَحَدٌ ۞

In the name of Allah, Most Gracious, Most Merciful

1. Say: "I seek refuge with the Lord of the daybreak."	﴿قُلْ اَعُوْذُ بِرَبِّ الْفَلَقِ۝
2. "From the evil of that which He created."	مِنْ شَرِّ مَا خَلَقَ۝
3. "And from the evil of the darkness when it spreads."	وَ مِنْ شَرِّ غَاسِقٍ اِذَا وَقَبَ۝
4. "And from the evil of the blowers into knots."	وَمِنْ شَرِّ النَّفّٰثٰتِ فِي الْعُقَدِ۝
5. "And from the evil of an envious one when he envies."	وَمِنْ شَرِّ حَاسِدٍ اِذَا حَسَدَ۝

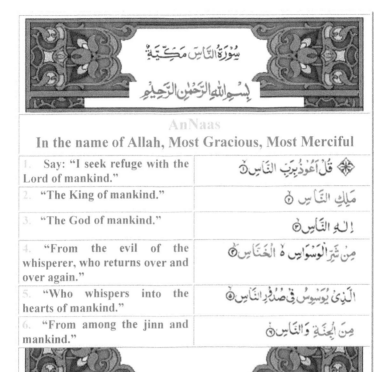

سُوْرَةُ النَّاسِ مَكِّيَّةٌ

بِسْمِ اللهِ الرَّحْمٰنِ الرَّحِيْمِ

AnNaas

In the name of Allah, Most Gracious, Most Merciful

1. Say: "I seek refuge with the Lord of mankind."	قُلْ اَعُوْذُ بِرَبِّ النَّاسِ ۞
2. "The King of mankind."	مَلِكِ النَّاسِ ۞
3. "The God of mankind."	إِلٰهِ النَّاسِ ۞
4. "From the evil of the whisperer, who returns over and over again."	مِنْ شَرِّ الْوَسْوَاسِ ۞ الْخَنَّاسِ ۞
5. "Who whispers into the hearts of mankind."	الَّذِيْ يُوَسْوِسُ فِيْ صُدُوْرِ النَّاسِ ۞
6. "From among the jinn and mankind."	مِنَ الْجِنَّةِ وَالنَّاسِ ۞

Lightning Source UK Ltd.
Milton Keynes UK
UKHW021527120920
369688UK00003B/54